The Bouquet Race: Chapter 9 Smile, Don't Grin

The Bouquet Race: Chapter 9

Smile, Don’t Grin

by Noble Lee Lester

10,637 words

7033 Cavalier Rd
Jacksonville, FL 32208
(904) 895-0162
nobleomagie@hotmail.com

ISBN:
979882443747

DEDICATION

To all the bygone ancestry, who for whatever reason God deem them fit, landed by coercion on this continent, for the sole purpose to work for free in a political land that advocates the right of liberty and gladly take death, I write this novel to those arrested that they in some way receive thanks for all their struggles. Their efforts not to destroy this nation but to dignify this land's statue for freedom was not a waste. Yet, as they observe ongoing degradation of being colored and ill-guided wishes to lift their voices, self-esteem and bootstraps.

I want to thank Dave Chatterton for being an inspiring and perfect living example of a customer service person and GM for Historic Tours of America from whom I gleaned many of these customer service skills. Not a day did he leave home without his understanding smile, kindness, and diplomacy and how that best influenced his managing staff. Thank you for being the boss of a decade.

And more solidly, I want to thank all the tireless efforts of great Black women in America for standing up, walking tall and lifting their chins to the solidarity of Black Lives Matter. You and the recent sacrifice of George Floyd, in the words of his baby child, "Saved the world." I salute you great leaders for your service. Now, I see your work and results everywhere. Again, thank you.

Contents

PRELUDE TO A SMILE 15

BUBBLE-GUM PHILOSOPHY? 17

There's power in a smile from black faces—any face 18

What happens when you don't smile? 23

Remember you are not just grinning 25

BUSINESS AND FAMILY (Same thing) 29

Don't refer to black entrepreneurs, guests, patrons or customers as "girrlll," chiiild, "dawg," bruh, or "my niggah" 30

Black and White restaurant distinctions: lying photos 33

Customer service is basic manners 36

LaQuisha, the customer is "stupid!" But they are always right, dear 39

Overcome objections: don't suck your teeth, bitch or moan 41

Understand the situation (and don't act-a-fool) 43

PUBLIC PRESENTATION (Black Lives do Matter) 45

Is your "defense mechanism" always set to: pissed-off? 46

Don't eat in front of guests (close your mouth at least) 48

Never "drink" in front of customers (don't burp at least) 52

Avoid being so dam loud 54

Attitude is everything, Miss Cotillion Debutante 56

Direct customers to other sources 58

Stage face..60
Greet er'body wif warmth and kindness (even da' bitches) .63
Be open and connected (not just your knees, heart also).....65
Define your customer's need (even da' bitches) 67
Show them your passion (Other than praisin' da Lord).........69
Give people the whole pickle: Fix it.......................................71
Texting sensitivity (eggplants, peaches, hanging cherries)....72
A LITTLE SELF-IMPROVEMENT? (It won't hurt) 73
Don't let anything get to you: Again, no one can piss you off--we allow that..74
Watch your tone ("What?!" Can be confrontational)............76
Apologize and acknowledge your error (...didn't hear you...)78
Red balloon..80
Warm goodbyes are just as valuable as greetings.................83
What the f...! Ghetto plexiglass? 90
Be grateful for any business or gift (*God leases hands*).........94
You (How to play Karma) 95

A Prelude (from my father):

This book (The Bouquet Race series: Smile, don't grin) is a series of chapter pieces about Black people—African Americans-inspired by my dad, Steve Lester, who didn't particularly favor the various race titles, names, epithets, and descriptions given to us/him during his time (1920 thru 2010). He had an amazing culture shock shared with my mother, Seanna, during their honeymoon trip in Atlanta, Ga. in the 1940's. They not only met "beautiful lookin' Negro peoples" everywhere but unlike most of the rural areas of Valdosta, Georgia, and Thomasville Alabama, where they were from, at that time, were also highly educated, professional, and socially refined in African cultures. He never forgot those unprecedented civil anomalies; African oddities to him if you will, "these beautiful, good-looking peoples" in that way he would address them. What did he see so different, so pure and refined? Perhaps their dignity shining through, their relishing of freedom to be, do and go where they pleased? He was so astonished he thought he'd privately rename them different from the national labels they'd been inappropriately called to "The Bouquet Race." He'd deed something he thought more deserving that he hadn't seen in the local "Negro or Colored People" he grew up among.

My father would often say, “Negro peoples is like a bouquet of flowers, Nobah. We are all different; all kind of colors and shapes.” Like my father, I am not a spokesman for shades and hues of Black people, but I am an appreciator of the misrepresented cultures they hail from, and all the influences left to me.

What is this book about? How to love Black people.

I figured if White majority Americans and former President T…. would go quasi-Nazi nuts after mulatto quarterback Colin Kaepernick took a knee in protest of safety, freedom and serve pledged white policemen killing Black boys, women and children in playgrounds and pool parties, Blacks could use some love.

When the phrase "Black Lives Matter" made majority White American's disregard our cry with, "All Lives Matter" or Blue Lives Matter," clearly, they are not willing to hear our cry-out for love. So, what is Plan B? Perhaps bubblegum philosophies like this book where the appreciation we lack is on us to provide.

I thank you in advance for reading this series of 9 books, "The Bouquet Race," codifying the many aspects of Black and White cultures and conflicts in America and sharing my father's sentiments and my empirically raw wisdom.

Chapter 9

POEM

My wife shows me a picture and says, “Now that’s a smile. So smile fo’ real!”

I say, “I am smiling.”

She says, “No that’s a grin. Smile. You have a beautiful smile. A handsome smile.”

I argue, “I am behind these eyes and this face. I don’t know what I look like.”

She says, “What makes you smile?”

“When I see you.”

“Well, think of me before you take the picture.”

“But I might start to cry.”

“Why?”

“I don’t know. I guess I love you so much you bring too much joy to my heart.”

“...Now, you gon’ make me cry. Well, try to smile, but don’t grin, baby. You have a lovely smile that moves the room.”

#

Figure 1My G-dad & G-Mom Orson and Leila Barfield

- <u>***Proverbs 15:13-14***</u> *A merry heart maketh a cheerful countenance: but by sorrow of the heart the spirit is broken. The heart of him that hath understanding seeketh knowledge: but the mouth of fools feedeth on foolishness.*

- <u>***Proverbs 17:22***</u> *A merry heart doeth good like a medicine: but a broken spirit drieth the bones.*

#

PRELUDE TO A SMILE

As for trends, we all can agree that smiling during a time such as this is not intrinsically practical. Trends are things that people follow because they don't have a sense of self or importance. A grin in such a time is understandable because we aren't genuinely happy. Happy days for now are gone. America was never happy but more guilty. They covered it with alcohol, drugs, gambling and eating junk foods to cover the guilt of having killed off Native-Indian children, fighting the British, enslaving Africans, taking land from the Mexicans, colonizing Hawaii, trying to fix a French war lost with Napalm Bombs; daring Coloreds, Negroes and Afro-Americans right to sit in a tacky Woolworth and go to some state colleges of their choice. So, a grin is about as much as we can do now in a divided democracy where we've chosen gangsters, bullies, and crooks to be our congressional members in hopes they will play out as the gunslingers of the wild west once did to take back something they were responsible for screwing up initially.

I get it. There is no amount of "sorries," justice and reparation that can make us forgive reckless, ill-servicing police and Klan racist judges to get African Americans to smile willingly from the heart.

I get it. With all the horrendous oppression done to Blacks, finding a "Satchmo" or Cab Calloway smile on our faces, that White America might feel less afraid, less threatened, and comfortable is challenging. In fact, I think Mr. Callaway and Louie were simply grinning to get through the hour.

BUBBLE-GUM PHILOSOPHY?

There's power in a smile from black faces—any face

Why do you think white people are so relax when visiting the Caribbean?

The power of a kind and welcoming smile is hard to feel threatened by. It lures a spirit in everyone particularly Europeans. They feel charmed, accepted and more importantly safe. It is the very thing that Blacks in America have long for as well, a feeling of national safety, acceptance, and friendship.

This Photo by Unknown Author is licensed under CC BY-NC-ND

Unfortunately, here in America, a black face represents fear to whites as well as some blacks. Sadly, too many whites, obviously not all, are subconsciously, and consciously, reminded of all the horrible things their ancestry has done to Negroes, People of Colors and Native Americans. Look at the political promises of late to remove Black History from the school curriculum. It's not that it all didn't happen or let's look at it differently, but let's pretend it never happened entirely. They suffer horribly from the guilt of it where they don't want their kids shamed and reminding them of their past to present racist behavior. Can you imagine at the dinner table Johnny wants to know, "Why did you do such a thing to my friend's family? What monsters you are." Any child of a guilty racist would dread to hear that.

Their fear is not that you won't fit in, flow, or connect with them but they fear they won't connect with you and by trying too hard they'll upset you. It's terribly stressing for them to fight for political correctness. And that feeling might be their fault too they fret from too many years of excluding Blacks, ignoring their culture, stealing Negro recipes, and calling it Southern Cuisine, recruiting their males' athletics when you NEEDED TO WIN, and red lining them into specific neighborhoods and school districts when they needed to pretend Blacks didn't exist. Not to

leave out, the waste of good melanin on the poor class.

I don't mean to be cruel or harsh and go out too far, but I can't phantom the cause of this deeply driven hate to abuse and undermine African Americans and people of color in general. White South-Africa apartheid absolutely lost their minds here. I have thought long and hard on this enslaving phenomenon. It makes no sense to me to have Blacks to work for whites for free when there were unemployed Grapes-of-wrath Caucasian people living in the sheltering woods and forest. And even today, there are more fenced in trailer parks spread across these united states then there are ghettos and slums.

Again, I am not trying to be mean by misrepresenting anyone, but enough racist behavior toward “inferior” blacks are enough. You are right, “All Lives

Matter." It's just a shame Blacks must remind whites of that in a free democracy.

<u>I've left room for notes</u>

What happens when you don't smile?

Unless a domestic animal has a memory of kindness from a human, they are less likely to trust and approach a human. Unfortunately, this is how many whites react to Blacks until they smile. If Blacks don't smile initially, anxiety is stirred in them that they can't readily read your below the skin disposition, thoughts, and feelings. Flash your pearly whites. There is something about that against dark colored skin that's simply sexy. You remember Sidney Poitier whenever he smiled?

Take care of your teeth so people can see your health. They represent a large part of your good looks. Look, gold teeth are very cool if they are selectively and conservatively placed, but a full gold grill, in my opinion, can look intimidating and hideous. A smile can disarm a policeman, relax an HR rep, charm a girlfriend, and cause grandma to emote, “Come, baby give nanna a kiss.” I get it. Many blacks don’t get a lot of chances to REALLY smile from the heart. What, with police shootings, jobs suddenly filled upon Black application, solicitation, and affirmation-action and reparations being laughed at, it’s a wonder Blacks aren’t growling in church.

Remember you are not just grinning

Look, the "Yass sur, boss man" days are over. There once was a time I observed my dad's oddly passive behavior toward whites, doing such a thing to feed us, keep us out of warns way, and keep us accustomed to which we were accustomed.

Steve Lester (Center pic) was a boy born of the southern 1920's to which I won't fill in his Dixieland atrocities incurred. Unlikely many northerners and southerners today, who vote against black racist history, I'll let your imagination fill in and rubric-cube what his pretentious grinning had to accomplish. Women might not leave home without lipstick, but men of his era never left without their "yass sur" grin. Observe:

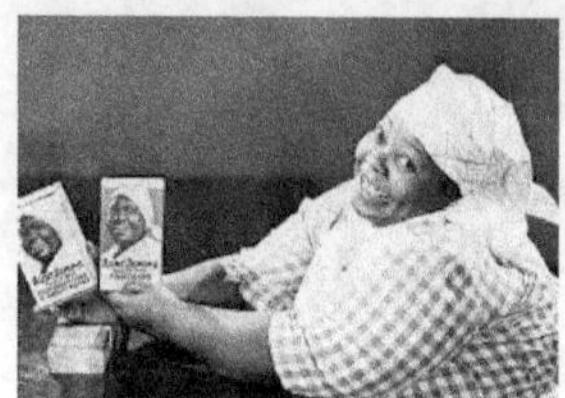

Little BLACK SAMBO

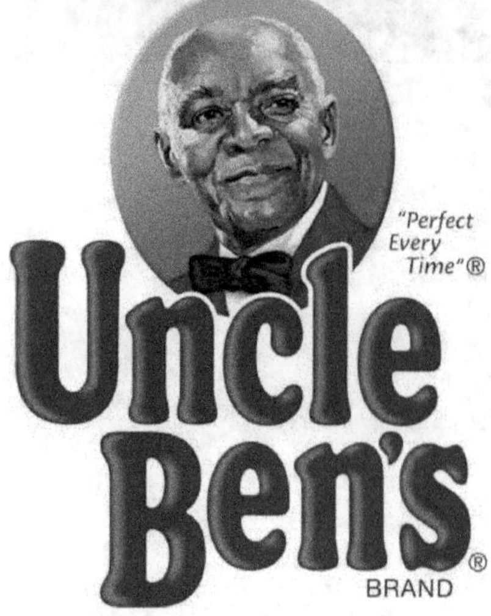

Faces fashioned to not intimidate or threaten but calm the savage beast in their oppressor.

BUSINESS AND FAMILY (Same thing)

Don't refer to black entrepreneurs, guests, patrons or customers as "girrlll," chiilld, "dawg," bruh, or "my niggah"

Let's not diminish decorum, etiquette and formal manner when doing business with astute clientele and honorable mentions. Trans-respect should not be limited to church authority and clergy. Respect must be extended even in common and general environments. Salutation to a "brother" on the streets will get you gold street credit. Give them the time of day too.

400 years of loose courtesy to one another has left us to be common, "regular-peoples," and plain-o-colored folk. No dammit! That's enough of that! Yes sir, and no ma'am, should always be a canon-greet and a proper regard--no matter the dress code or unconventional demeanor. Let's us rid ourselves some of these antiquated ill-mannered regards and begin to dignify each other with heightened common courtesy. Because once upon a time, when overseers, plantation owners and the American government saw you as 2/5th a person, you should never let them, or see yourself, in that way or other Africans like you. Certainly, God never saw you that way. Why? Because everything you touch is a song. It shows brilliant whether you are dressing, ball playing, cooking, preaching, teaching,

or counting the galaxies or the stars, you exult. God has given you the spiritual wherewithal to-do-it-to-death.

Okay, I get it. It appears you think you have an affinity for me because I'm Black. So, in too many cases, some salespeople, who are black, want to common our relationship with unnecessary commonalities. It would be like a red-neck through an arm around Queen Elizabeth to express a buddy o' pal-dom on a sister. "Past-da-jelly-plz." Approach with dignity and integrity, and perhaps sometime later one might wait for the cue to venture into "kool-colloquialisms" when deem permissive. Once the business is satisfied, rectified, and solidified, there we can break out da' BBQ, brown paper bag 40oz, and the crab-boil.

No dammit, you are not being bougie because you want the numbers to add up and everybody holding down their station. We must gain solid self-respect, and love of self. Once that adheres to the stone and the gospel, all satelliting want-a-be's will want to join and be a part of your grandeur.

My stepdad Cleveland Raymond taught me, "Keep some cash in your pocket, education in your head and the love of God in your heart and EVERYBODY WILL call you Mister.

Commonalities, like such, come with other colloquial idioms that middle-class Blacks don't like to be reduced to but taken seriously and to ascertain a feeling you see the importance of respect and honor and you are a working part of the game. Successful Blacks have worked hard for their gains. They want to know, that you know, the party and celebration begins when the game is won, over, and the ring is achieved. My niggah, my dawg, and my main man comes later.

<u>I've left room for notes</u>

Black and White restaurant distinctions: lying photos

Black people and most people of color, like every creature on this planet, has a defense mechanism. Generally, Blacks run, duke-it-out with their hands, run-back any field, dunk the ball for the key, put her hands on her hips, roll-her-eyes, suck her teeth with intimidation and puff-up and stare you down. Blacks generally don't use subliminal psychology, but they'll make a bully laugh to minimize an eminent ass-whupping.

White people on the other hand have a defense mechanism of persuasion and propaganda. Their defense is articulated charm, entrapment, psyche-motivation, and posse ganging. For example, corporate whites concentrate on image; a delicious appearing food item to stimulate one's mind/pallet for psychologically suggestion; an image to override the actual lacking aroma, warmth, and taste. Is Taco Bell real Mexican food?

For Blacks, it is not that black restaurants, don't have the budget for advertisements—of course, some do. But Black restaurants are focused on the aroma, warmth and magic in the taste and flavors in a dish; not mind-game illusions and food mirages.

This Photo by Unknown Author is licensed under CC BY-SA-NC

This Photo by Unknown Author is licensed under CC BY

Blacks say, "The hell with trick photography and staged images but lip-lap on some of dis. Child, I can't eat no pictures." There lies their magic.

I witnessed a disappointed date at Red Lobster after the couple received their dwarfed lobster dish. Not trying to spoil his date, the big fella' beckon for the waitress. When she arrived, he politely said, "Would you take this back and bring me the menu picture." Clearly, the rustic looking boyfriend was deceived by the restaurant's artistry leaving a much to be desired actual seafood dish.

<u>I've left room for notes</u>

Customer service is basic manners

Smile even though your heart is breaking, being under paid or if your feet are hurting from a long day.

Yes, for years I have criticized black store owners of their grimacing faces, daring looks and mean expressions. Their pretentious, resentful and under rehearsed, *"May I help you, please?!"* I didn't understand until I too began trying to sell my own wares. I felt black people's lack of support and absent awareness of the "stick-with-it" angered me knowing they wouldn't buy anything, tip, or worse, support me out of pity. That would make it hard to be warm and friendly or no sale or no sale would occur if any. Therefore, I had a negative attitude toward their pretensions and misgivings.

Find in yourself the feeling of pride you've worked hard to serve others and bring them pleasure in their restaurant experience or whatever experience. There is much to ascertain when you do your best to be your best. There is ALWAYS a blessing waiting around the corner to thank you for a work well done. No, I am not trying to persuade you back to some Aunt Jemina pearly-white grin-hard tactic. Let's go back to the days when "darkies" were "so happy" and grinning broadly.

No. let's not. Hell no. Just bring pride to your work and good service to others. This is how you build a dynasty the people can't EVER forget. The blessings you long for lie dormant inside yourself. The gate key is not passiveness, denial or defensiveness but confident service and willingness to assist.

My dad, Steve Lester said, "I don't care what you do. Just be the best at it."

Pride in your work is what the world will admire. "If you find something you love to do, you'll never work a day in your life."

<u>I've left room for notes</u>

LaQuisha, the customer is "stupid!" But they are always right, dear

Sure, I am always right as a customer. Their ego comes first. The salesperson's job is to please and charm me that I never feel contradicted but ushered down a path of betterment of new knowledge.

White cultures in America have an encroaching proclivity to believe people of color have an inferiority to their bombastic avalanche of questions they equate as superior intelligence. What they generally do not understand about themselves is their bombarding fears that urges them to over think and second guess everything and body until they find satisfaction deflating their anxiety based on their awareness and approval of the availing answer.

In other words, they won't calm down until the answer to their fears feels or sounds reasonable, logical or like something they'd linguistically approve of.

To get what you want from this "customer" one must know they are skeptical of you only because their culture has convinced them of such dating back to their pre-school years. Your only weapon for success, the sale or getting on board is your smile. Not your grin. Find in your heart to win by accepting them as a person. They generally feel lonely and powerless, but your smile says you could be my pal right here and right now.

<u>I've left room for notes</u>

Overcome objections: don't suck your teeth, bitch or moan

Never argued or fight with a disgruntle, fussing or objecting customer especially when other customers are about and within ear shot. If the customers are white, you don't have to disparage. Typically, and this is awful I know, but if other Black customers are about, they might wait around to see the fight escalate before rising to your defense. (I'll talk about that behavior later) However, typically for whites, the second you choose to conflict with an irate and irrational red neck (or some dick), you will lose. As long as other whites see that you're trying to deescalate the rising temperature, generally they will try to overcome the dick's angst civilly. They will step to your defense and perhaps even bounce them and throw their ass to the pavement. All for you, provided you're that smiler they trust. When white people see an inkling of passiveness, calm, and soft-spoken behavior in a black person, they want to become your rescuing calvary.

Why this fear vs a smiles phenomenon so whites feel an alliance, an alloy toward Blacks? This book isn't about socio-psycho analysis but survival among people who find security in white skinned humans rather than a harmony and trust in all species of human mammals. It is what it is? It appears that chromophobia and xenophobia is a real threat for some white Americans. Why do they suffer so? I don't know. But Gene Roddenberry and George Lucas have tried their darndest to depict a universe filled with oddities some getting along and others, not so much. But nevertheless, they showed diversity in the vast stars.

I've left room for notes

Understand the situation (and don't act-a-fool)

Whether your customers are white or black always pull out the stops to please them in business. "Give them the pickle" which is a good old business adage where you always give them something more that pleases them with extra, or more importantly, it shows the customer you genuinely care. Forget about tips, a good sell, or a perfect hookup that favors the customer, can only serve you in the long run. A selfish businessperson is soon to depart from his money. Believe it: When an effort is made from earnestness, only good can follow that. The Universe serves the giver. Why, because that's what the universe asks of mother nature that she gives, loves, and rejoice unceasingly.

I am an orange tree grower and every orange that I pick to eat the tree buds' extra flowers for oranges come the next season. You can only know this when you live with the tree year to year.

You see, karma is real. What goes around comes around. As long as we/you/I love mother nature she'll reward us with abundance.

This Photo bv Unknown Author is licensed under CC BY-NC-

I grow datil peppers for my hot sauce business and every morning I pick the fruitiest bright yellow pepper right at its maturity, and ironically the next morning there is a rewarding cup fill from each bush. The plants seem to enjoy providing fruit for the picker. It seems to want to help and give more by giving more each year. I believe it's the way God set the universe and I think it'd be healthy for us to follow suit as the world turns to complete the day, the month, the season, the decades, and the centuries. What you give the customer extra will return to you multiplied.

PUBLIC PRESENTATION (Black Lives do Matter)

Is your "defense mechanism" always set to: pissed-off?

Generally, too often, Black people are too ready to fight attitudinally, argumentatively, and unfortunately with physical violence. Having your attitude cocked at "pissed-off" is never a profitable, politically or a good thing. A good attitude is like a genuine compliment that makes your friends and customers feel good wanting more.

Okay, if anyone I don't know calls me out by saying, "I'm a bitch" typically I might be riled-up to be offended and retaliate with a rash of mean words or foul sounding comebacks. But the reality is "The Bitch Caller" never provoked me as much as I provoked myself giving me permission to never tolerate such an insult remedying it with perhaps something violent--no, she/he/they didn't make you mad, or hurt you. You gave permission to self. This is an overused example, but rappers call each other and their audience, Niggahs" all the time. And we give ourselves permission to accept the insult as an endearment. And there is no violence provoked or annoyed because it is endearing.

Simply put, no one makes you mad, angry, or pissed. No one. Really. Pay attention to your feelings especially when you are trying to get something you need, want or desire. Getting pissed-off is a staged emotion retort for them. Fuck that! Your emotions should be about you and yours and the success you need. Piss smells. Success is lasting and looks good in the bank.

I've left room for notes

Don't eat in front of guests (close your mouth at least)

Don't eat in front of me when making a deal unless we're at lunch meeting or a company BBQ where it is appropriate. Let the black or white customer know or at least think they are be held in high esteem...respectfully. Oh, and spit out your dam gum.

All this loose common behavior is not because Blacks are bad, lazy, or inferior. When 6 million Black people migrated amass to the north after reconstruction, there were not much of a collective social system, other than the church. There, they might learn to dress nice, hold themselves in esteem and stand tall and ready to die for their families—and their "country." Blacks were treated like animals for so long some began to think that of themselves. They would generalize and diminish themselves with labels like, "A niggah ain't shit." Their societal job was not to mandate the protocol of business but be the workhorse who finalized the plan—and they be the muscle. So, they kicked rocks repressively and act-a-fool until their orders were handed down.

They seldom ate lean potions of meat of any kind—some didn't even prefer it. They got used to rationed so-called slop, swine by-products, pig ears, neck bones, pig feet, tails, and hogshead cheese delicacies.

This Photo by Unknown Author is licensed under CC BY-SA

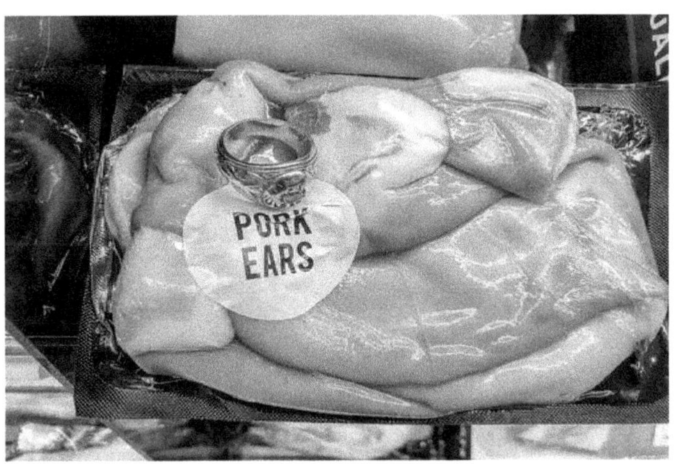

This Photo by Unknown Author is licensed under CC BY-NC-ND

This Photo by Unknown Author is licensed under CC BY-NC-ND

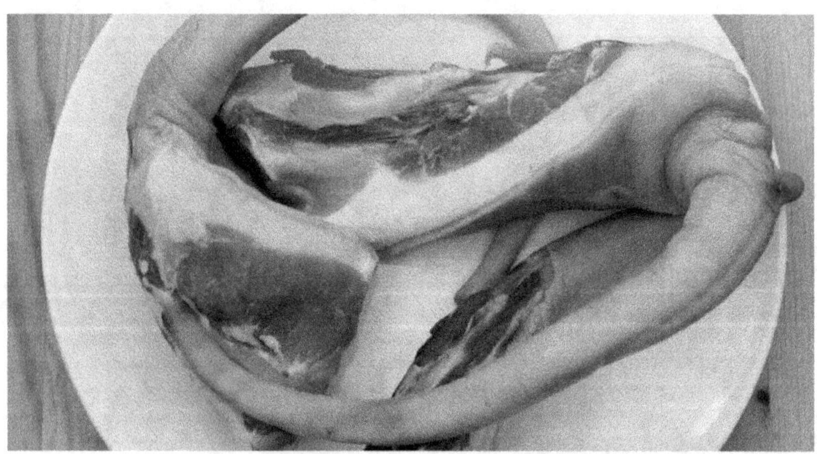

This Photo by Unknown Author is licensed under CC BY-NC-ND

This Photo by Unknown Author is licensed under CC BY-NC

Many Blacks were dignified and found their way, but a lot didn't, leaving them to be wild, reckless and spiritless drifters.

Never "drink" in front of customers (don't burp at least)

Ditto, yet again, much like the previous bullet point like eating in front of clients, customers or solicited leads, don't drink alcohol. A light wine at the luncheon or pop a beer later, and even then, where appropriate, never brown bag a 40 ounce

when addressing a customer or closing a deal. If they offer a scotch, sip on it like its battery acid. Close the freakin' deal with a sober head. Your Gatorade splash and champaign will wait.

<u>I've left room for notes</u>

Avoid being so dam loud

Loud means, you wish all attention on you—the center of attention—AJ's: attention junkies. It also means you have a vast competition issue where feelings of inferiority and validation is not present in your world or earlier in your life. Or you're just a big-hearted Leo or Libra who's bursting with a song in your soul to share the world. Again, loud only works for someone else who's performing—on stage. There, larger than life is expected. Even inside the theatre, as audience members, people don't necessarily appreciate your loud ass commenting on the action. I know white people don't like it; hell, it pisses me off too. Generally, movies are romantic atmospheres, a date. Pre-COVID-19 was a place lovers could sit close, be in the dark, massage body parts under the popcorn bucket. The live stage theatre is indeed about class and respect for the live performers. As for comedians, don't say shit but laugh—remember you aren't mic'd. No one cares. Take the comic's insult, move on fatty. Treat public venues like your grandmother taught you to hush in church—or she'd slap the taste out cha' mouth, "You heah?!" It's the same inadvertent public respect you want. Convincing the world that Black Lives Matter starts with these above tactics. Yes, you are your brother's keeper; not givin'-a-fuck is bad PR for your black-family—

especially your imitating children. However, do be loud in the stadium. The players need the encouragement.

<u>I've left room for notes</u>

Attitude is everything, Miss Cotillion Debutante

NYC Italians were famous for calling out a "freakin' attitude." Some nerve! No one had a worst disposition than they. It was their excuse to break some freakin' kneecaps.

Black people can be billionaires tomorrow if only they check their attitudes. A smile attracts wealth, prosperity, dates, friendship extra food from waiters and cooks. A sweet disposition brings about angels and money. Highway exit beggars never get much money because they often don't smile. They solicit the drivers with a facial attitude, "You owe me."

A smile, along with some like good humor, people just want to be around you. What late night talk host greets their audience with a pug face. Sure, you can be aloof and off to yourself but always smile as people pass your gauge with a gentle smile. If someone wants to engage you with conversation listen. Listening has the power of intelligence. A fact: when you listen, people think you're conscientious and they will label you intelligent. Talk less and listen more. You do not have to be a member of their ideologies or BS to listen. And, if your done with them, thank them and excuse yourself with a smile. "My God, look at the time!!" Take care of your teeth or put your dentures in because a warm smile is money in the bank and changes everybody's first impression of you and all you represent. A smile makes Black Lives really Matter.

<u>I've left room for notes</u>

Direct customers to other sources

When you don't have the answer or the thing they need, be ready refer them to other sources. Service to others is like a good virus karma that continues to come back to you plentifully—it's like a cornucopia--a gift that just appears. It's an invisible angel that will follow you attracting things and people to assist you, connect you and be da' hook-up for you. It's how good marriages work; two people giving and giving with no motive of gains or returns, or you owe me this or that.

NEVER blow anyone off because their interest doesn't serve you. You got the time...take the dam time. Lend a hand, an ear or some two-cent advice. It might account for millions to the other guy or girl. There is ALWAYS a ram in the Bengal bush Los Angeles.

ALWAYS be of service. Making people happy will make you happier. Try it. That's what performance is all about. It's all that pleasure giving to their audience where they find themselves, the performer, feeling cosmic love in return.

Knowledge sharing is a service. Hip-a-brother, pull someone's coat or lend a hack or a tip. We all know something the other guy might not be aware of. If you have it, give ‘em the scoop—the heads-up. It’ll all karma back to you.

I’ve left room for notes

Stage face

A stage face should never be a grin. Look, being positive is not being a Cheshire-cat looming in the corner grinnin', or noddin' like an Uncle Tom. Being positive is to avoid negative thinking and feeling inside yourself. This positive shit is HARD as the dickens. Trying to remain positive is challenging. However, DO NOT spend anytime criticizing how others should behave less negatively. That is just a way of masking your own negativity. Negativity is their business and their cancer and to be perfectly honest with you there isn't a great deal you can do to relieve them of their funk. To many people, being, talking and feeling negative is natural—it feels real to them. Some will tell you, "I'm just bein' for real."

Prolific cussing or potty mouth people will laugh and smile in the same breath. What they fail to realize is cussing is a spiritual regurgitation of deeply seated hurt, pain, and resentment that swells up where people have not, or unconsciously, unwilling to forgive past traumas and hurtful bullies.

It is hard to forgive. People will tell you they understand that forgiveness is a release valve for themselves, but most people feel it's letting the other guy (the offender(s)) off the hook; that they are getting away with something. The forgiveness is for you to get you off the hook of pain, anger, and resentment some just can't seem to shake. Most people for one reason or another carry a chip on their shoulder about something or someone who did them wrong. And there's secondary chipping; the kind you carry for the other guy, family or friend whom you don't even know. That's the worst chip on your shoulder—somebody's other dirty laundry.

Yes, negativity eats at us. It devours our goodness, joy and fun. Because bliss awaits us all but negative "cleaning" has to happen before bliss can break free of the cocoon it's entombed in.

Sure, everybody's got to bring their game face; their 9:00 am Monday morning perky sunshine freakin' grinny face; with an evangelistic upbeat voice to boot. We all hate the dam pretentious "good morning" BS. I have fantasize telling people at work, especially my boss, "to fuck off. Leave me the hell alone until my coffee kicks in or I mentally wake-up around 11:00 am." "Go somewhere and kill yourself, thank you very much."

I get it. And I'm not telling you to change that. But I'm afraid, that Black people can't do what white people do. Unfortunately, and that day will change, Black people will someday be regarded as privileged Americans. Thanks to mixed marriages and their mulatto children. It's just a matter of time, MLK, Jr. Oh, some have it but it ain't a culture in corporate America just yet. We still got a little-bit-mo’ smiling to do before we get there—I have a dream too.

I’ve left room for notes

Greet er'body wif warmth and kindness (even da' bitches)

Instigators are hellhounds. They are the enemy of the people, or Grinch, stealing your peace and filling their base with mass misinformation. Don't waste time with them but reserve your rewarding smiles. They wouldn't know a smile if it kissed them. For example, shock-jocks, they're people with deep rooted flaws that will use your kindness for weakness. Believe it or not, they are outnumbered. There are more good people than bad asses in the world. It just appears the bad asses somehow need and want the microphone a lot eagerly than the decent.

This Photo by Unknown Author is licensed under CC BY-ND

When was the last time you heard the Dali Lama bitch about a cracker or a niggah? Or, Martin Luther King speech whining about investments and cash flow? Instigators are deeply hurt people and they want everyone to hurt with them. Instead of improving, changing and evolving they know only to add to your misery to company theirs.

<u>I've left room for notes</u>

Be open and connected (not just your knees, heart also)

To be more open is not necessarily revealing one's business but looked at positively it's a way of ascertaining more information. Exchanging info is paramount. Learning about the world around you is mental expansion. To grow bored with info is to limit your knowledge, your thoughts and having an educated base to form a sound opinion.

Ants are magnificent communicators. Every numbered length and intervals while traveling they leave a marker, perhaps embedded by a scent. In that marker, the ants leave several inherit notes of information where they've been, how far they've traveled, food benefits and discoveries, any unfortunate dangers, and exact locations. Hence, the ant farm is wholly supplied with a wealth of information they all can and will benefit from. To be turned off or bored with knowledge and information other than negative tidbits is communally dangerous and unforthcoming.

On a spiritual tip, information is like education and being educated is to get closer with God. What or who knows more than God? What's more brilliant than God. What's more positive than God? It is when we expand our horizons with information which is what education is; we align ourselves with God. To know the stars and the depth of the ocean is to open the channels of euphoria. So, be open and connect with people. They can be your ocean and stars fill with wealth of knowledge and inspiration. People can be God's thoughts, voice and feelings. It is my belief God uses the heart of people to bless us or each because He has no hands, but he has us to pass along His charities.

I get it. God's "so-called blessings" can appear untimely, cruel, and non-existing. Religion can mislead us to get jaded when God is not that at all. However, a sanctuary or venue is convenient to gather in faith and prayer. But God is something else entirely. In my opinion, God is in our thoughts and visions. The world has plenty of words hence endless prayers, but feelings and visions are His read that He might make that which you believe manifest. Everything was a thought before it grows, developed, or manifested. See your smiles. Feel the love.

Define your customer's need (even da' bitches)

When you've learned to connect, be open and sensitize yourself to the people's needs, you can win anything from anyone. When you are white, you can be as mean as the Yev Kassem, The Soup Nazi from Manhattan, NYC (a real commercial soup kitchen) who will chastise and harass his customers if they are fussy, pushy, impatient, or attitudinal, he will put them out with no soup. And the White patrons will return again and again for more of his abuse. Jerry Steinfeld and his crew returned again and again.

Below pic, this is early morning closed shop photo on west 54th St between Broadway and 8th St. Seinfeld made a mint depicting this soup chef character on his comedy show.

St. Augustine's beautiful Spanish historical grounds doesn't bother white people's lack of heritage if it appeals to be white influenced, white managed and white curated exploiting Sthe ancient history. As long as you do not mention the extermination and genocide of the Timucuan Indians pre-the Spanish colonization, and later the purchase of Florida eradicating the Spanish of their property and heritage. Or, the Old Jail sport

hangings (lynching's) of Negroes at the Old Jail or the Fort Moses black calvary who fought back the encroaching French and multitude of pirates while the Old Castillo Fort was being constructed in 1672. You can sell ANYTHING with a warm smile and an intelligent sounding voice. Yes, I did say "sounding." I'll talk more later.

Show them your passion (Other than praisin' da Lord)

White people love to hear from Black people when they've bought into their political BS. For example, how great America is than any country on the globe, thanking soldiers for their service, singing the national anthem without taking a knee in police brutality and murder toward Black men and women, shouting out the pledge of allegiance, prefixing and addressing Capitol Hill incumbent elects with "the honorable" and "sir." Politics make their dicks hard. So, be like James Brown when he sang, "Living in America." Mind you, if you study his lyrics, James only mentions cities in the lyrics in America where Black people have thrived and are concentrated. No, he did not mention, Boston, Tulsa OK, Birmingham Alabama or Charleston SC.

Ray Charles, "Georgia," i.e., *Georgia on my mind* was a double entendre superimposed by the state senate of Georgia to obviously represent that particular state and all its grandeur. But, your boy Ray Charles, and song writers Carmichael and Gorrell), initially directed to the romance of said woman who was royally and sexually on his/their minds.

Look, Georgia on my mind was an endearment given to Ray was from that state made from a proper pollical opportunity to address the goat of Rhythm and Blues as a peace offering to the world given the post racial times in 1979.

<u>I've left room for notes</u>

Give people the whole pickle: Fix it

I cannot reiterate the "pickle" enough.

When I was a child growing up in South Trenton, New Jersey, I learned many good habits from the surrounding Jewish communities. Unfortunately, during those times Jews were heavily redlined and discriminated by Protestants and Catholic whites just like Negroes and Coloreds. Yes, in the north, they were redlined into specific city areas. They would hem-n-haw and lament with my father about antisemitic systems that block them from expanding politically and economically. Their pickled tomatoes and gefilte fish odors weren't embraced back then by Whites. But, among themselves and their allies, like my family, they were fond of "giving their customers the (extra) pickle." When they served, for example, a Reuben or pastrami sandwich on rye they would serve the customer with a quarter of a pickle. But if a customer asked for more, they'd get the whole thing; not just the regular patrons but all whom they'd serve.

Remember that giving is a way of the world. Rainfalls never cease. Sunshine never fades and the seasons always change. The earth is always serving us something different, yet the same, and giving us more of it. Life can be the whole pickle if we but enjoyed our gifts with love and a great smiling thanks.

Texting sensitivity (eggplants, peaches, hanging cherries)

Words and images in a text can be dangerous. It only depends on whose reading and how you feel about that person. To someone you love, and they love you, you can send lude emojis, and even physical pics. That might be perfectly fine to the consenting, receptive party. But, to a person that doesn't want you, like you, or have NO intentions for you, could be dangerously offensive and lead to something horribly irreversible. No, this is not an experience of my own, but I've heard "tail."

That's an extreme miss use of inappropriate sensitivity, but simple misunderstood words, phrases and unclear thoughts can lure people to me offended and misled. Be careful with what and how you say with assuming words.

Lives have been destroyed over self-assumed intentions and poor truncated English and misunderstood acronyms. Equally, be careful with emojis. An eggplant can be delicious in a lasagna dish but that coupled with a donut-hole could get you in jail; if exposed inappropriately. They can send messages that can put you and Hilary Clinton in the same doghouse.

Keep the language of text in a complimentary mode of communication. Keep things short and sweet. I find most people aren't talented enough with words to say anything beyond a couple of sentences. Any negativity is a FaceBook death sentence.

A LITTLE SELF-IMPROVEMENT? (It won't hurt)

Don't let anything get to you: Again, no one can piss you off--we allow that

Of course, we'll talk more about tone of voice and how impacting that can be later. But, for now, no one makes you mad especially something "they" said. Really. We only decide that what was said cause me to fire up my anger. ***I fire up my own anger***. If someone calls me a lover, that might sound nice. I can choose to be flattered, shy or boastful with "That's all?" If someone calls me a genius, that might feel good too. But, typically, if someone non-black calls me a niggah, temperamentally I might prepare to be jailed for assault—justifying battery or murder. On the other typical hand, when a rap song, or family member or friend so-call reference me their niggah, I decide to be less volatile and embrace it endearingly. No, the circumstance ain't "different, doh."

This is a biggie for black women especially: If someone calls them a "bitch"... STOP. Put on brakes. NO, don't take your earrings off and step out your heels. Simply make the decision that you aren't a bitch, or niggah, and walk on to live better, happier, and freer yet for another day. True freedom starts with you and your self-applied ability to control yourself and YOUR feelings. This is not bubble-gum philosophy. This responsibility is life or death. Give yourself the permission to choose is paramount. Julius

Caesar was right about one thing: “The fault dear Brutus is not in our stars but in ourselves.”

I’ve left room for notes

Watch your tone ("What?!" Can be confrontational)

People like to philosophize about how one should talk to women, elders, one's mother and be mindful of your tone of voice. I think that applies to everyone. Men are also taken by the wrong tone. I hear many Mafia-boss have taken consequential action from a poorly expressed mouth. Whether whom you're talking to is a child or an authority, everyone deserves respect and common courtesy. One should never limit decency to teachers and clergy but be kind to everyone especially people who has some influence on your lifestyle, success and length of life.

It was a mid-range lesson I learned from my adopted mother, Seanna Sally Lester. A child DID NOT reply, "What!" to a parent callout. You said, definitively, and with total absence of defiance and projected annoyance, "Yes ma'am." I have been slapped for my tone of voice and perceived disrespect.

Currently, police are still shooting and beating Black men and mouthy women for their perceived disrespect of the law. Their racist disposition takes it upon themselves to punish and reprimand the inferior who don't know the power of their pre-judgement. However, it is the welfare of Blacks to learn to smile and deescalate the ignorance of the puffed-up lawman, and in many cases, law women who forget they are only law enforcement not the deeming prosecution or judgement of the alleged broken law.

<u>I've left room for notes</u>

Apologize and acknowledge your error (...didn't hear you...)

Don't let apologies get too old. Look, some people forgive instantly, and others might brew a lifetime. Waiting for your family or friend to apologize first is a show of your arrogance. Tough guys in this case get very little but a great deal of regret. Arrogance is a stonewall to stubborn to move—or admit fault. Old hubris has the context of great Greek dramas. Religiously, we all know who got thrown out of heaven for being arrogant and haughty. There's no asset there unless you like tossing and turning all night long alone--pretending you don't care. I think the leading cause of death is arrogance. Why, because arrogance causes inner stress and stress kills. Simple equation.

Making yourself believe it was his fault anyway—"cause I didn't do anything." So, until you admit you're the faulting cause, I'll just mentally-block my whole life and brew, brew and stew, stew. Stupid, stupid, stupid. Look at it this way, apologizing is not a show of weakness but a credit for sleepless nights, and feelings of loneliness.

I wonder, when all is shot down and blown apart, how will Vladimir Putin hold up after all the shattered families, and pissed-off oligarchies, are tallied, all the funerals have shifted to a lifetime of grieving and the world forever spits in his face. Will he apologize, Caesar? Or will he buddy up with George Zimmer and OJ Simpson and share some poisoned Kool-Aid? Apologize now before karma visits with a spoil you'll forever regret.

<u>I've left room for notes</u>

Red balloon

When an angry, frustrated or disappointed person is blowing off steam, try to imagine their head to be that of a fully inflated red balloon.

This Photo by Unknown Author is licensed under CC

From an observing audience point of view listen to them and try not to engage, respond, or defend your opinion or side of the story but let them shout it all out. Imagined the red balloon deflating. Listen as long as you can suffer it; patience here is a virtue. Eventually the balloon will deflate, and often they will calm down afterwhile having gotten it off their chest. They will more than likely become reasonable and after a smile will think the world of you. The trick is your ability to mute long enough to let them exhale all their toxin disappointments and ill feelings. This is NOT EASY guys.

Like any humans, a customer ranting and raving makes the serviceperson (you) feel guilty, accused—the blame—where you might wish to fight back or get rid the complaining "belly-acher" with some equally strong words. No ego wants to feel like a chump. So, a couple word-jabs might satisfy their self-esteem having retorted or retaliated with a harsh rebuttal.

But no, what is gained. The game here is to win and train oneself to be bigger and stronger to see anger for what it is. Hot air.

Remember, the customer is always right LaQuisha. You really don't have to get a jackass straight to feel noble. That kind of action is a lose-lose action. Be wise and let the balloon deflate and give them the pickle they never get from this harsh money hungry world they are probably struggling with; or a privileged jackass who's never learned gratitude or the power of faith and patience. But you ma'am, sir, gave them some extra stuff, a welcome smile, an opened ear, your "upmost" attention and your patience.

I am sorry but no one wins with a get-a-niggah straight, open a can-of-whoop ass or bitch-slap the taste-out-your-mouth" action. These satisfactions are short lived and long consequence. Proof? Black Americans made up roughly 72% of incarceration rates. A shame before God.

<u>I've left room for notes</u>

Warm goodbyes are just as valuable as greetings

Warm greetings are a matter of an attitude adjustment. One must learn how to want, or at lease desire, to make people happy and welcome in your presence.

Okay, I get it. You live in a fucked-up world where white people have screwed people of color over for hundreds of years. Yes, your grimacing contempt looks are justified, and like Mount Rushmore, are solidly engraved in your countenance. Hiding the truth of one's feelings is hard for the heart and face. Those are the two things you don't see in yourself like others see on you. Much like a happy puppy never sees its tail. If the puppy loves you, there's it's swag to show it but if it despises you, you will see its teeth. Both, he's not entirely aware of vs your grin to your smile.

And then again, The Undisputed Truth of Motown sang, 1971

Smiling Faces Sometimes tell lies and I got proof.

Smiling faces sometimes pretend to be your friend.

Smiling faces show no traces of the evil that lurks within.

Smiling faces, Smiling Faces, Sometimes they don't tell the truth.

Smiling faces, smiling faces tell lies and I got proof.

The truth is in the eye 'cause the eyes don't lie, amen.

Remember, a smile is just a frown turned upside down my friend.

So, hear me when I'm saying

Smiling faces, Smiling Faces, Sometimes they don't tell the truth.

Smiling faces, smiling faces tell lies and I got proof.

Beware. Beware of the handshake that hides the snake,

I'm tellin' you beware of the pat on the back it just might hold you back.

Jealousy, (Jealousy) misery, (misery) envy.

I tell you you can't see behind

Smiling faces, Smiling Faces, Sometimes they don't tell the truth.

Smiling faces, smiling faces tell lies and I got proof.

Your enemy won't do you no harm, 'cause you'll know where he's comin' from;

don't let the handshake and the smile fool ya.

Take my advice I'm only tryin' to school ya.

Smiling faces, Smiling Faces, Sometimes they don't tell the truth.

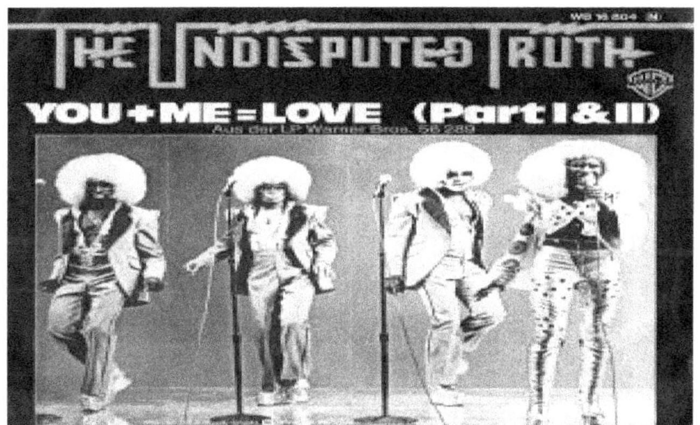

This Photo by Unknown Author is licensed under CC BY-SA-NC

They were singing to a Black audience. And there again, Black people still suffer aged to ancient distrust toward each other innately for the many sellouts, snitches and assisted slavery imports. Perhaps intrinsically, Africans never forgave ancient brethren—slave catchers. There had to be. Black men have been known since Jack Johnson to Floyd Mayweather to whoop-ass. There is no way an average size 5′ 4″ Spanish men and Ricket suffering pale cancer prone white cracker under African sunlight haul millions of Niger dwellers out of their habitat without a scuffle or two. Even Black women and children will royally kick your ass; I've seen my mother do it. So, let the truth be told snitch-filled resentment among Blacks.

But who suffers the most by your lack of smiles and resentful anger? You do. Show business giants had to learn to hone and master their performing arts skills and talents but they also had to appeal to their cruel audience no matter how fucked up with superiority and racism white jack asses behaved or how cruel Blacks were at booing new unestablished talent off stage and control their passions.

Motown, as well as Stax Records, was rigorous, hardnose and task driven about getting it right and rising to perfection. They had to also ace charm school techniques like articulation, table etiquettes, dress, walk, talk, how to interview and treat their public before they went on tour.

The Green Book was unknown to White people across the south—and north—but Blacks had to move and travel like Harriet Tubman in the early 20th century up and down interstate highways. Blacks had to literally learn how to be invisible around White people although celebrity.

This Photo bv Unknown Author is licensed under

The Green Book was unknown to many Negroes. Again, like Mrs. Tubman, celebrities couldn't afford snitchers trying to gain clout with racist Whites.

Show business blacks had to KNOW where they could eat and sleep. Get their money upfront and look for a back door and escape car while crackers got "shit-faced" and drunk. I am not suggesting you put up with anymore of their racial sickness but just learn how to survive and win. Win. Remember this: what is your goal with them? Do you want to debate them, back-n-forth, fight, prove something to yourself, or get paid and enjoy your family and friends for another day?

Again, this self-hate thing that blacks have for each other stems from snitching. There is a real cause behind old adages like, "A niggah ain't shit" which stems from tattle telling informants. Black people for 400 plus years had a hard time from whites who saw them as animals and equally fellow blacks who saw them as expendable and worth tattling on to ascertain some fantasy clout with white people. It's never been white people's nature to care for foreigners unless they were white and superior minded. They saw their opaque ghostly flesh as a token of superiority with a privilege to do whatever they please. And, before they had blacks to rule over, they abusively ruled their own poor, infirmed, old and sexually different. Why do you think there has to be legislative laws in place to force respect for gays, trans, the old and sickly and black civil rights? These "humans" aren't trends. There have been gays since the beginning of time. Why laws? Because they are reckless and too weak to stand on a principal of decency and do the right thing.

To this racist mindset, a warm goodbye supersedes their second guessing of your competence. A white managed store generally suffers no second-guessing notions about returns regarding to their rustic roadside culture. They will spread 5-star reviews toward their Hillbilly hustle. However, for you, as long as your warm smile escorts them out of the door, your good and you'll make the sell. The "smile" worked for Nat King Cole.

What the f...! Ghetto plexiglass?

Don't go into another freakin' plexi-glass business establishment. Fuck them. Oh, I get it. I know why there's plexiglass in all the corner stores and gas stations in the "hood." Well, there is the obvious COVID-19 defense. Granted. But plexiglass guards existed long before our pandemic. Okay, there's the obvious thieves, robbers, and needed physical protection. That's real. I get it scary-ass clerks need to feel safe—but at the cost of your customer's dignity and respect? But nowhere have I seen plexiglass with exception of the "hood." Even, top class to middle class black neighborhoods have plexiglass issues. Again, I get their fear and their need for caution but what about their neighbors' esteem. The store owner, generally, white, Arab, some Black or Asians seem to fear the same when it comes to us blacks. I say, be done with them. I know, it's a normalcy now. Some blacks don't even see the glass barriers. They've accepted the labeling stigma placed upon them: A NIGGAH WALL. You are not to be chanced or trusted? Let's think this thing through: There was a times when drug-heads and crack-addicted junkies would indeed do anything for cash to get their fix on. How does a crackhead ascertain such a firewall crowning? Perhaps by legal importing of such opioids and contraband across borders. Who's supplying these product demands. Who is getting these duty-free illegal substances and drugs to and fro the borders and state lines?

Who's ultimately responsible? Who are these bountiful importers? People who, perhaps, have the wherewithal of masked shipping, connections where the item(s) are processed and sold? Or own the proper geographic UV light zoning where these illegal substances might easily grow. Okay, mangos don't grow in New Jersey. So, the equator connection where these items/produce do grow must have a sanction of entre.

Get it? Someone, or conglomerate corporation(s), with the necessary funding and payoff money to deliver the product to market causing crackhead contingency and need for plexiglass is a shame. I am not going to lay out all the operational moving parts to paint you a better picture with evidence. But we know those people, or operators, take on entities like ICE, ATF and the DEA whose job is to flush out and seize these illegal importations aren't as successfully as one would hope having landed prolifically in da' "hood" with great success. Now, I ask you, having your imagination filled in the missing puzzle pieces, does that sound like a crack-head operator business behavior and capability? And, to boot, what we get from such brilliant risk-taking drug maneuvers are a resulting plexiglass in our high or low in class neighborhoods. This "normalcy" must stop yesterday. Tolerating a NIGGAH WALL? You got to be kiddin'.

I've left room for notes

Be grateful for any business or gift (*God leases hands*)

Remember that blessings MUST be administered through hands. Since God doesn't have any, He uses His inhabitance to deliver His gifts—using you and me. So, it might be more important than some casual nod to return a proper thank you so that more blessings will follow.

Not everyone will like you but there's nothing to stop you from regarding them with decency and an accepting smile. George Wallace (The comedian) says, "I love you and ain't a dam thing you can do about it."

Show your gratitude with an amazing attitude so that the messenger who delivered the gift returns with love from me to you. Thank you carries a power. People feel appreciated, regarded that their free effort, time, and money didn't go to poor use. Similarly, when you borrow money and pay it back, more important than banks, loved ones will love you for it and represent your sense of responsibility at the Thanksgiving table. What you don't want is the scourge of "hustler" circling that same table. That is the table of judgement when you don't pay back that which you owe. Loan-sharks have been known to kill instead of waiting for their money. God is pretty clear about debts, bartering, usury and theft. It ain't good.

Be gratefully thankful.

You (How to play Karma)

Yes, this a face that only a mother could love. With that frown, whew, she might have her doubts also—bless his heart.

What is a smile. It can be both a verb and a noun. "A **smile** forms one's features into a pleased, kind, or amused expression, typically with the corners of the mouth turned up and the front teeth exposed." –Cortana, 2022.

If Vladimir Putin smiled right now it wouldn't mean shit. Like other current and historical dictators' smiles are timely and when we humans failed to understand its power for good it can expire on you never to be used for endearment of any kind. Those turned up lip-corners with flashing pearly whites (even gums) are invaluable to relaxing, welcoming, approving, encouraging, and loving has the power blessing and crowning.

Black folk, Indian folk, and American women, I get it. Sometimes with all the bullshit you've endured and put up with is painstaking to eke out a real smile of bliss and joy. I know. I know. You don't like faking your feelings. Not asking you to. But think about those times when you have genuinely smiled from the heart, cried tears of joy and belly-laughed to the point of breathlessness. Those moments have amazing efforts on everybody. Where everybody wants a piece of that Lovejoy, they can't resist the act of smiling and laughing along with you or others. That's power.

Hear this, your smile doesn't make you a punk, passive or inferior. The smile gets you what you want and hopefully in time it'll become innate and natural to your world, your family and more importantly your spouse and children.

As I write this, Ukraine is under attack of Oligarch loving dictator, Vladimir Putin, who knows no such power of a baby's smile, a happy grandma with her grands or innocent young people giggling. And now, Putin will never know. He has forfeited this blessing. He is property of evil where nothing smiles, and nothing will. Nothing but grins will escort his last days. I pray that is not nor ever will be you, caught without a smile.

A smile is good Karma. It all comes back to you.

In the words of my dear wife, "Now that's a smile, Noble!"

Ecstasy Dining Room

AMAZING

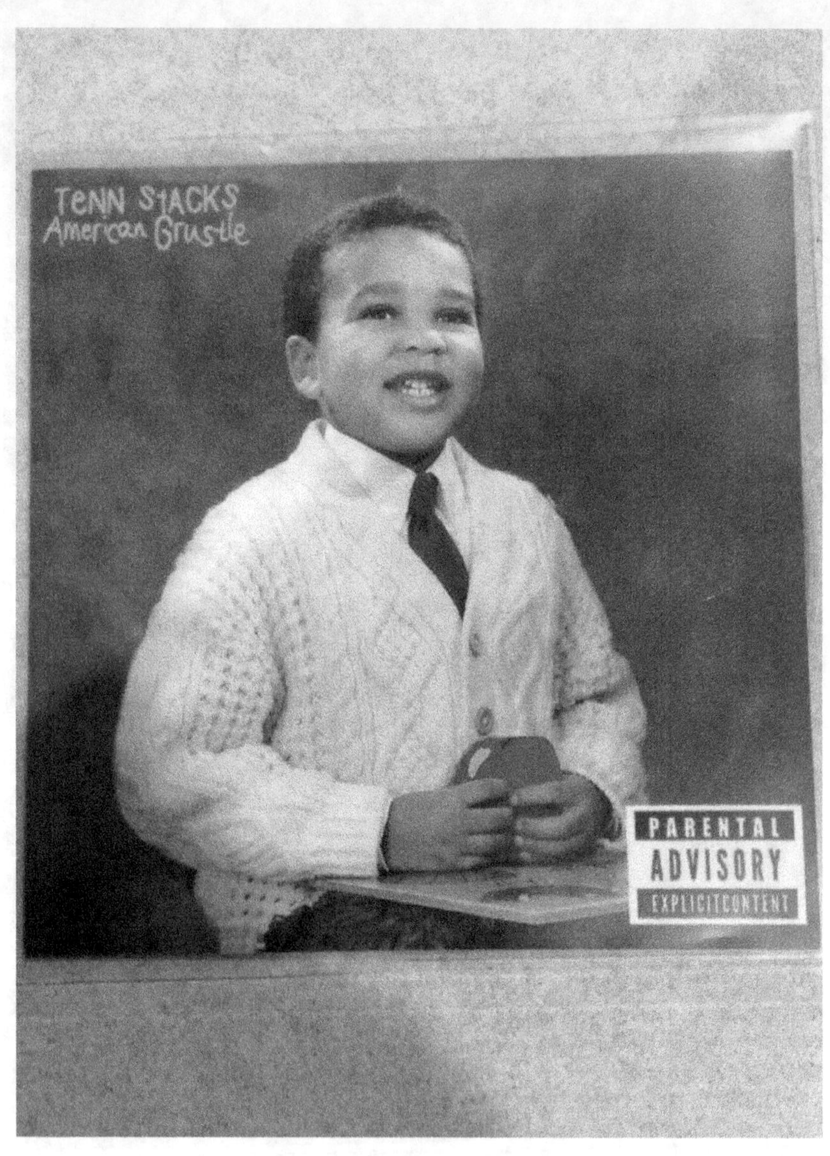
TeNN STACKS
American Grustle
PARENTAL
ADVISORY
EXPLICIT CONTENT

NIKE

MORE NOTES

www.ingramcontent.com/pod-product-compliance
Lightning Source LLC
LaVergne TN
LVHW012114160826
845678LV00014B/3090
* 9 7 9 8 8 2 2 4 4 3 7 4 7 *